THE BALD EAGLE
All About the American Symbol

by Tamra B. Orr

PEBBLE
a capstone imprint

Pebble Explore is published by Pebble, an imprint of Capstone.
1710 Roe Crest Drive
North Mankato, Minnesota 56003
www.capstonepub.com

Library of Congress Cataloging-in-Publication Data is available on the Library of Congress website.
ISBN 978-1-9771-2587-3 (library binding)
ISBN 978-1-9771-2607-8 (eBook PDF)
Summary: Arguably, no symbol more firmly represents our country's independence than the bald eagle. But why this particular bird? Young report writers will learn how the United States came to embrace this feathered American icon.

Image Credits
Alamy: The Picture Art Collection, 10; Library of Congress: 8, 19, 20; Line of Battle Enterprise: 7; National Archives and Records Administration: 11, 15; Newscom: Its About Light, 27; Shutterstock: Andrea Izzotti, 4, chrisdorney, 29, DnDavis, cover, Ellen Kowallis, 13, Feng Yu, 12, FloridaStock, 25, Jim Cumming, 18, jo Crebbin, 24, ket-le (banner), back cover and throughout, Krumpelman Photography, 23, Michael Shake, 28, Mikhail Hoika, 9, Paul Reeves Photography, 26, Peter Wey, 5, Steve Collender, 1, wholly macro, 21, Yaroslaff, 16; Smithsonian American Art Museum: Gift of Mrs. Joseph Harrison, Jr., 17

Editorial Credits
Editor: Jill Kalz; Designer: Juliette Peters; Media Researcher: Svetlana Zhurkin; Production Specialist: Laura Manthe

Our very special thanks to Kealy Gordon, Product Development Manager; Paige Towler; and the following at Smithsonian Enterprises: Jill Corcoran, Director, Licensed Publishing; Brigid Ferraro, Vice President, Consumer and Education Products; and Carol LeBlanc, President, Smithsonian Enterprises.

All internet sites appearing in back matter were available and accurate when this book was sent to press.

Printed in the United States of America.
PA117

Table of Contents

Words in **bold** are in the glossary.

Introduction

The United States of America has many **symbols**. Our flag is one of them. So is the Statue of Liberty. They are objects that stand for our country. The bald eagle is also one of those symbols.

Eagles are large, mighty birds. They are strong and fast. For thousands of years, they have been signs of power. How did the bald eagle become an American symbol? The idea goes back more than 200 years.

Try, Try Again

Before the United States was a country, it was 13 **colonies**. Great Britain ruled them. Many colonists were unhappy with British rule. So, in 1776, they started the **Revolutionary War**. They were led by a group called the **Founding Fathers**. Benjamin Franklin, Thomas Jefferson, and John Adams were part of this group.

As a new country, the United States would need a government. It would need rules.

Colonists fighting British soldiers (shown in red) during a Revolutionary War battle

Franklin, Jefferson, and Adams got right to work. One of their jobs was to design a **seal**. The seal would appear on all **documents** from the U.S. government.

Left to right: Benjamin Franklin, John Adams, Thomas Jefferson

Franklin and Jefferson wanted pictures from the Bible on the seal. Adams wanted the strong Greek hero Hercules. The men asked others for help. Everyone had ideas. But none of the ideas was quite right.

The Greek hero Hercules fighting a nine-headed sea monster

Finally, Charles Thomson was asked to help with the seal. Thomson was also a Founding Father. He was known as a smart, truthful leader.

Thomson looked at everyone's drawings. One had a bald eagle. But Thomson thought the eagle in the drawing was too small. So, he drew a new one. This one was big!

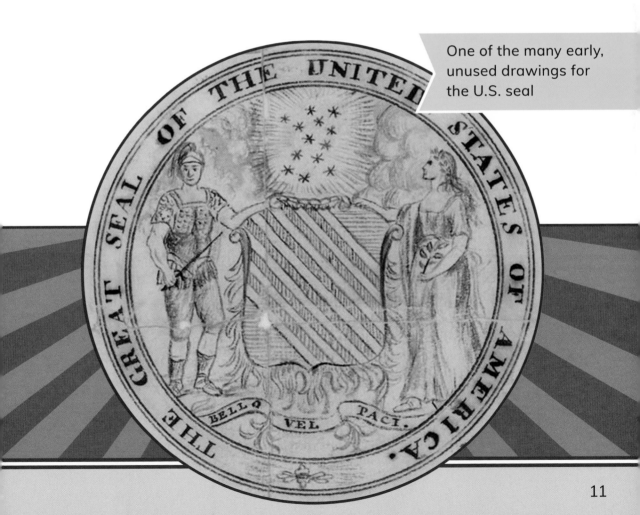

One of the many early, unused drawings for the U.S. seal

The Right Choice

Thomson knew that the bald eagle was the right choice for the U.S. seal. He had heard a Revolutionary War story about the birds. During a battle, the sounds of fighting woke some bald eagles. The birds flew down and circled over the American soldiers, crying loudly. When the men saw the birds, they shouted, "They are **shrieking** for freedom!"

Thomson's seal was approved in 1782. It showed a bald eagle with its wings spread. The bird's chest had a **shield** on it. The shield's 13 red and white stripes stood for the original colonies. The eagle held arrows, as a sign of war. It also held an olive branch, as a sign of peace.

The bird's beak held a long piece of paper. On it were the Latin words *E Pluribus Unum*. They mean "Out of Many, One."

Proud and Strong

Thomson was not the first person
to use the eagle as a symbol. People
around the world had used it for
thousands of years. The eagle
meant bravery, power, or wisdom.

An eagle and the god
Zeus on a coin from
ancient Greece

The ancient Greeks thought the eagle was sent to them by the god Zeus. Aztec rulers in Mexico added eagle feathers to their thrones. The feathers showed that these men were strong. Many American Indian nations believe eagles have special powers.

A chief from the Sioux Nation wearing eagle feathers

A Turkey? Really?

In 1787, the government made the bald eagle the **emblem** of the United States. Many people were happy. Benjamin Franklin, however, was not so sure. There is a story that says he wanted a turkey instead!

This story is only partly true. Franklin did write that the turkey was a braver, better bird than the bald eagle. But he didn't want it to stand for the country. He agreed that the eagle was the best emblem for the United States.

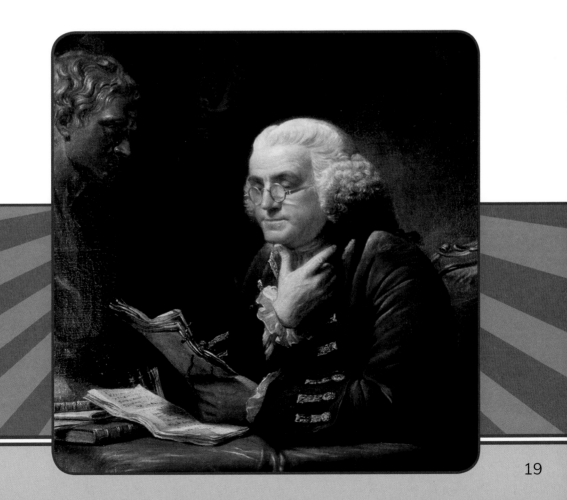

In Danger

Soon, the bald eagle appeared on U.S. money. Some states put it on their flags. Over the next 100 years, its strength as a symbol grew. In 1961, President John F. Kennedy wrote a letter about the bald eagle. He said the Founding Fathers had picked the right symbol. The bird stood for "the strength and freedom of America."

But the actual birds were in trouble.
Long ago, thousands of bald eagles
lived in North America. By 1963, only
about 800 were left.

Americans worried that the bald eagle would disappear forever. They worked to try to save the bird.

The government helped. The Bald Eagle Protection Act was passed in 1940. In 1962, the government made it stronger. The act said it was against the law to catch a bald eagle. Next, a **pesticide** called DDT was outlawed. This poison harmed many animals, including eagles.

Today, the number of bald eagles is growing again.

An Amazing Bird

Bald eagles are amazing birds. They can live a long time in the wild—up to about 25 years.

From tip to tip, bald eagle wings may reach nearly 8 feet (2.4 meters). The birds fly about 30 miles (48 kilometers) per hour, on average. That is how fast cars go on many city streets. Bald eagles can dive through the air at nearly 100 miles (160 km) per hour!

Keeping Watch

Since the 1960s, Americans have been able to take a closer look at their national emblem. Thanks to video cameras, people can learn more about bald eagles in the wild.

Special "nest cams" have been set
up in the United States. The cameras
look at bald eagle nests. People can
go online and see the eagles lay their
eggs. They can watch the chicks hatch.

Near and Far

The bald eagle is a strong symbol of the United States. It appears on countless things, from our money and flags to clothing and cars. The bald eagle stands for power and freedom.

In 1969, the symbol even traveled into space. The **lunar module** for the Apollo 11 mission was named "Eagle." The mission's clothing patch showed a bald eagle landing on the moon. The bird carried an olive branch in its claws. It came in peace!

Glossary

colony (KAH-luh-nee)—an area that has been settled by people from another country; a colony is ruled by another country

document (DAHK-yuh-muhnt)—a piece of paper that contains important information

emblem (EM-bluhm)—a symbol for a country

Founding Father (FOWN-ding FAH-thur)—one of the men who created the U.S. government

lunar module (LOO-nuhr MAH-jool)—a small vehicle used for traveling between the moon's surface and a spacecraft

pesticide (PESS-tuh-syd)—a poison used to kill insects and other creatures that are harmful to plants

Revolutionary War (rev-uh-LOO-shun-air-ee WOR)—(1775–1783) the American colonies' fight for freedom from Great Britain; the colonies later became the United States of America

seal (SEEL)—a design put on a document to show it is approved by a certain country, state, or group

shield (SHEELD)—a flat object that protects a body

shriek (SHREEK)—to scream or yell loudly

symbol (SIM-buhl)—a design or an object that stands for something else

Read More

Bailey, Jill, and David Burnie. *Birds*. New York: DK Publishing, 2017.

Ferguson, Melissa. *American Symbols: What You Need to Know*. North Mankato, MN: Capstone Press, 2018.

Marcovitz, Hal. *Bald Eagle: The Story of Our National Bird*. Philadelphia, PA: Mason Crest, 2015.

Internet Sites

American Bald Eagle Information
http://www.baldeagleinfo.com/eagle/eagle9.html

Enchanted Learning: All About the Bald Eagle
https://www.enchantedlearning.com/subjects/birds/info/Eagle.shtml

National Geographic Kids: Bald Eagle
https://kids.nationalgeographic.com/animals/birds/bald-eagle/

Index